AF228978

I'm Thinking of an Ocean Animal

Bela Davis

Abdo Kids Junior
is an Imprint of Abdo Kids
abdobooks.com

abdobooks.com

Published by Abdo Kids, a division of ABDO, P.O. Box 398166, Minneapolis, Minnesota 55439.
Copyright © 2025 by Abdo Consulting Group, Inc. International copyrights reserved in all countries.
No part of this book may be reproduced in any form without written permission from the publisher.
Abdo Kids Junior™ is a trademark and logo of Abdo Kids.

Printed in the United States of America, North Mankato, Minnesota.

052024

092024

Photo Credits: BluePlanetArchive.com, Getty Images, Shutterstock

Production Contributors: Teddy Borth, Jennie Forsberg, Grace Hansen

Design Contributors: Candice Keimig, Pakou Moua

Library of Congress Control Number: 2023948542

Publisher's Cataloging-in-Publication Data

Names: Davis, Bela, author.

Title: I'm thinking of an ocean animal / by Bela Davis

Description: Minneapolis, Minnesota : Abdo Kids, 2025 | Series: I'm thinking of an animal | Includes online
     resources and index.

Identifiers: ISBN 9798384900573 (lib. bdg.) | ISBN 9798384901273 (ebook) | ISBN 9798384901624
     (Read-to-me eBook)

Subjects: LCSH: Ocean animals--Juvenile literature. | Questions and answers--Juvenile literature. | Riddles-
     -Juvenile literature. | Sea life--Juvenile literature. | Animals--Juvenile literature. | Zoology--Juvenile
     literature.

Classification: DDC 591.92--dc23

Table of Contents

Guess the Animal!

I'm thinking of an ocean animal. Can you guess what it is?

I'm thinking of an animal
that breathes underwater.

6

But it is not a swordfish!

I'm thinking of an animal that lives near **coral reefs**.

8

But it is not an angelfish!

I'm thinking of an animal that eats crabs.

10

11

I'm thinking of an animal that is an **invertebrate**.

12

But it is not a lobster!

I'm thinking of an animal
that has arms.

14

15

I'm thinking of an animal
that shoots ink.

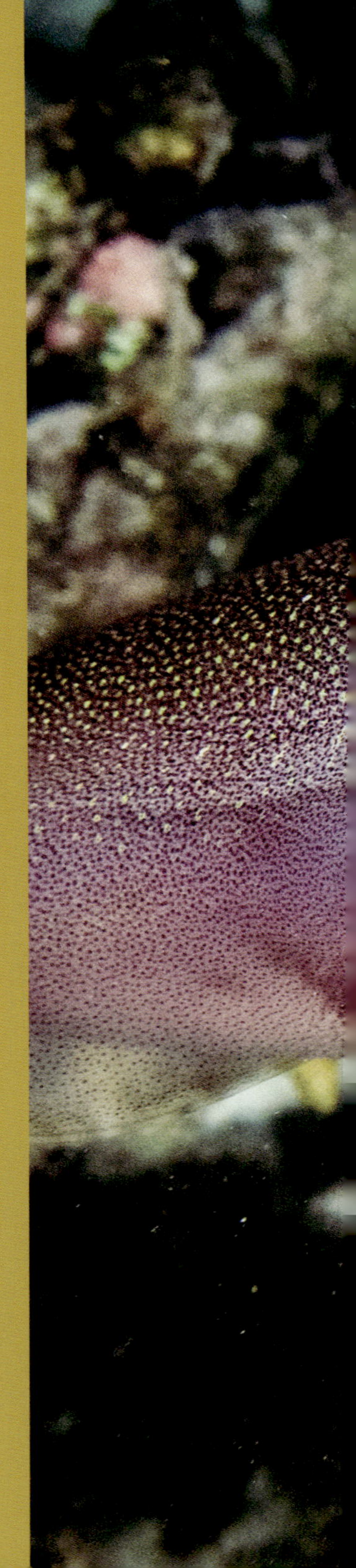

16

But it is not a squid!

Do you know what animal

I'm thinking of?

clues

- breathes underwater
- lives near coral reefs
- eats crabs
- invertebrate
- has arms
- shoots ink

18

19

I'm thinking of an octopus!
Now it's your turn! What
animal are you thinking of?

Comparing Animals

	angelfish	stingray	starfish	octopus
lives near coral reefs	✓	✓	✓	✓
eats crabs		✓	✓	✓
arms			✓	✓
shoots ink				✓

Glossary

coral reef

an underwater structure that is made up of the hard skeletons of tiny sea animals called corals.

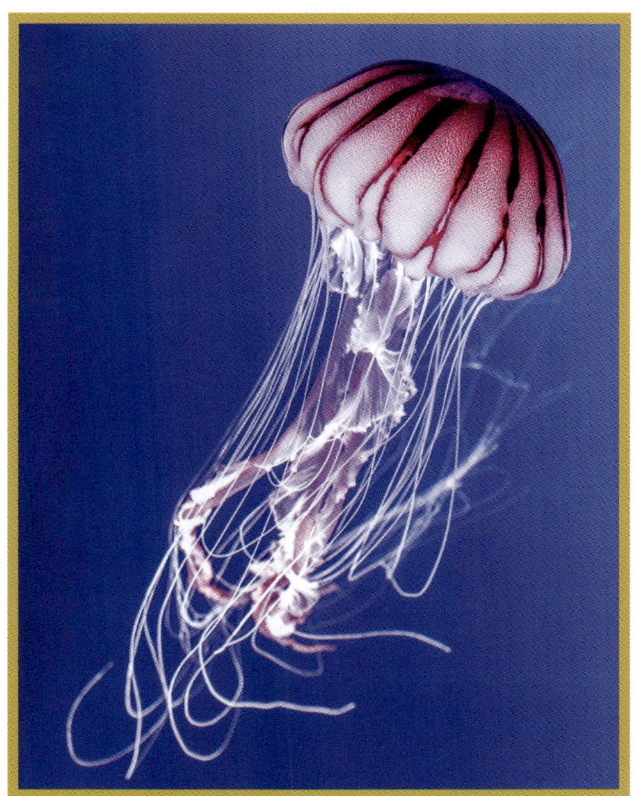

invertebrate

an animal that does not have a backbone or skeleton inside its body.

Index

Visit **abdokids.com** to access crafts, games, videos, and more!